Green Glasses

by Janice King

Freedom Voices
San Francisco, California
2000

The following poems have been previously published: A Man is Hardly Needed in *Burdens of Bliss;* The Lunch Date, Out of Control, and Short Life in *Tender Leaves;* Snowman in *The Haight Ashbury Literary Journal;* James Chin in *Autobiography Magazine;* The Daydream, *Oxygen;* Reno in the *Tenderloin Times;* The Car in *Processed World.* Peaches and Sixth Street are excerpted from King's unpublished and stolen book *Dial Designates.* My Father Killed Outdoors in the Morning is from the unpublished book *The Burning Biennium.*

Edited by Eric Robertson
Produced at Red Star Black Rose North in the U.S.A.
Cover and book design by Ben Clarke. Based on a drawing of a pair of green glasses by Alice Gould.

P.O. Box 423115 San Francisco, CA 94142
www.freedomvoices.org
info@freedomvoices.org
ISBN: 0915117-04-5

When I told a child she shouldn't be talking to a stranger, she replied, "*You're* not a stranger."

from *Jasmine for the Jazzman*
1974

CONTENTS

CONTENTS

A Man is Hardly Needed

a man is hardly needed in my life
gone are the days when i couldn't
get along without him
in my life a pillar like the sun
i leaned on and i died
when quietly alone

i am busy — without concerns
going two ways — alone
i shore up material goods just for one
and count this keeping in my room
a life — !

The Lunch Date

Across the street the shadows
make circular lace on the pavement
and sides of a building.

What am I to do, alone in a
small restaurant?

At the foot of a tree outside
a pigeon pecks his bride
shepherds her quickly, so quickly
then stops, diverted by a crumb.

Across the street two buses pull up
bright and loud as football players
I have no date for lunch or dinner
this poem is my date, lunch, dinner

a first time experience with prostitution

in a high cranky voice
you cried
about the people
that didn't like you
and your wife's suicide
you said you'd rather talk
  ten minutes was up
  suddenly you tore off your clothes
  and I had to apply myself
  i made you climax
  before you knew what you were
  going to do
i tricked you, to end it
you blamed me
i washed with urine like i was told to
and went downstairs to junius
  i gave him a dollar, kept nine
  and went to the corner store,
  bought fruit and cookies
  i had been **hungry** for days
junius with a cigar jutting up
he with the open friendly face
and a degree from UC Berkeley
where i had studied too
junius was breaking me in
  he drove me home in his car
  came over that night
  lit my candle and turned out the light
  and threw a fat shadow on the wall
that night i heard voices
and meandering bars of music
and urinated copiously
over and over again on the floor

Green Glasses

I saw green frames
seductive as Jade
carved into empty ovals
took a leap
into gamblers green water
popped out wearing
green glasses like a
touch of fashion
in the rainafter gleam
of Market Street hirizes
I saw the street for the
first time lens-correct
I have a paid-for passion
for green (last time
I needed glasses I got
city government discount).
Something about these
Jade ovals surpasses -
Green Glasses!

Dogtooth of the Rose

I have finished my work.   I thought
about population and the environment
I served a man his cake and soda
I wrote to two loves I am
going out into the night
to mail these letters
now I desire the dogtooth of the rose.

His face has a yellow cast
like light dust
and his tooth grazes his lower lip
even when his mouth is closed
and his tooth calls to me
when his mouth is open
when he tosses his head
his lips are full
they are like warm bread
O my God how I desire
        the dogtooth of the rose

All I met was a guard with a nightstick
I saw a few manikins with haircuts
but not the dogtooth of the rose.

In San Francisco in this Tenderloin
at Seventh and Market that gala market
I am still part Portuguese from Oakland
here, none to take me in his car
with the rough fellows
and stink of sour wine

Being Told To Do

He said look
I don't look
He says palms down
instead of palm to palm

My sister in his arms
my brother. He yells
Look. I don't look.
The nicotine floor,
it's a mirror of us smoking.

We fight
close to danger
but we are all right.

Puppets of what we have to do
we sing blue and cagey
what they told us to.

Out of Control

out of control
the roller blades hop the ledge
out of control
beer overflows the glasses
out of control
beauty of a woman
out of control
my ringing heart
like a bell
swinging
out of control

Fenton's

In Oakland, California
in the caves of Fenton's creamery
is the ghost of my failure to find love
I fix them with my eyes, the
swearing teenagers. my generation
did not swear so much.
       oblique ghost! failure.
A slant for fate
packed to bursting with
my silence. the glass seems cruel
while the teenagers drink opulent
milkshakes, the glass of coke only afforded
       and the failed visit. the gray plaster,
       bubblegum beaded
       entombs me in Fenton's caves
       and is cold
my narrow, bleeding fate
stuck me, an Oaklander, in San Francisco
to work, to heal, and to wait.
when I was a teenager, Fenton's
in Oakland was the hangout.

Field Burner

Birthday Cake Mountain
pines, cypress, pubic hairs
and the backs of necks so cute
shingled cone and the fragrant tops
the distance between me and Mom and Dad
an irrevocable distance with Brother
the kids think I'm inconsistent
so here I am far out in the cold
and it's my birthday! I take my torch,
my cigarette, begin to light
each pine and cypress.
Happy Birthday, here's your freedom
I climbed to the mountain's top and now
I begin to slide on the dry,
crumbling cake and the pines begin
to singe and the pines sing, Fire!
Fire! Now I'm at the bottom
of Birthday Cake Mountain
and I'm dirty. Smoke covers it
I can't make a wish and all there
is the next day are the bones of
desolate partying littering
and a disconsolate smell.
Did I learn my lessons well?
Yes. But it took a while
for the ethics of freedom and
burning to go home.

Facing the Attacker and Getting Red-Faced

I faced my attacker instead of turning my back to him.
He said he would kill me. He socked me like he would
a punching bag. I stayed in my abbreviated clothes
close to him. I did not dress and leave. I let him play
with me. I was so exasperated with his constantly
ordering me to adjust the radio that I left through the
door in my abbreviated
clothing. Out in the hall I could not go anywhere.
Finally he opened the door to the hall. "You went out
like that?" he asked. "Yes," I answered. He said,
"Then you will
have to leave." As I was getting away after he fell
asleep
I looked in his crudely framed mirror which sat on a
chair made of beat-up rustic wood.
All around my eyes (which had been punched) was a
bright pink.

The Conscience

25 broken scenarios
of approaching making love
but
I saw a stinking woodchuck
a skunk
heavy as a warning out of
Biology.
each stripe, each piece of fur
was a weakness or disease
from the Culture: their
bunnies, squirrels, beaver
rabbit and pig.

Hard Heart

His emotions caged
in a steely face
his words like an
unstoppable embrace
I want to stop.
It's unseemly.
His words aren't peerless
not of cosmic weight
but mistaken, dreamy.

Why can't he dream then
those solitary nerves
relax? Express
natural feelings?
The steel is an appeal
to me, an assumption
of eternity's firmness
over shakiness of mind.

But my heart's as hard
as an old Easter Egg
too old for eating
too poor for Fabergé

I let heart pass
in silence, lest I be
as well mistaken
as this guy is.

Heartbreak Hotel

I sleep with my money and keys
strapped to my body. That man
is still outside my door starving
me out. He knows no one comes here
in this mausoleum hall where he stands
with a knife, a scarf, and an erection.
He's already disconnected my electric buzzer
to the desk. But I have a piece
of wood my boy painted for me:
On both sides it says: WOMAN
IN DISTRESS! CALL THE COPS!
COME IMMEDIATELY TO NUMBER THREE EIGHTEEN
BLANK BLANK STREET! HELP! PHONE BLANK
BLANK
BLANK BLANK BLANK BLANK BLANK
and I 'm about to drop the piece of wood
three stories to the busy street below.

People Like You

For E.R.

People like you protect me
from People I don't know.
Stranger looks like so-and-so
and I emote from eyes and nose
the emotion I feel for you.
Stranger knows I'm thinking of him
as a particular kind of being
and so it goes as he acts accordingly?

I never met a stranger all anew —
they look like you and you and you —
you are good, they may not be
so I hold you close protecting me —
seeing a man with your face in the
train station — brought me up vividly
to a level of friendship with you —
not with him — you give me life.

The Ballad of Seesee Writer

Seesee Writer is a so-so writer
Literal, not writerly.
If the curses on his talent
Were verses out of his talent, he'd
Outstagger Stagolee.
Since his disposition's bearish
His penstrokes have no flourish,
And the questions in his brain are beggarly.
He has one redeeming feature
He can report an earthly creature
Just as it also looks to me.

Seesee's imagination would gain a higher station
Could it be taught to feel as well as see.

Who is Seesee Writer? It does not make me bitter
To report that Seesee Writer is part me.

The San Francisco Woman

The San Francisco Woman's style affected by modern
art
The Oakland Woman more sportsminded. The
Oakland look
Came to San Francisco as we held hands like bridges.
Huey Newton of Oakland gave us our relaxed curls.
We walk practical, in great big shoes and we don't fall.
We influenced New York and the media. We get
whistles.

The Flooding

At 44 McAllister Street one day in June
Unstopped water soaks through floors
Instant to the dining tables lies in lakes
11,000 gallons per minute crushing through
       fiberboard

Neither is my love contained: Here's my
       mud splattered kiss
My showers of bypassed gifts my excess
       my breakthrough

My big breasts made higher   burning
Pivot between legs   burning   all the way
       inside
Burning   an old woman's burning   It's late

Zones of wetted fire ignored   I do my work
Ignoring you   I do necessities ignoring us

And the dining room floor developed tides
Drying   lipped in dirt   in surly time

Which now is clean. After the busting of sprinkler
In empty room overflowing, I offer to you
My calm friendship sighing against flooding.

Rape Talk

I said
were you ever convicted?
That's right
I said, were you
ever convicted of rape?
Why do I? Because you remind
me of those guys that got
lovin somebody confused
with wantin to take
advantage of somebody.
Who me? No, I said,
oh yeh, there is an element
of wantin to take your advantage
when you do love
someone, but there's that
other different capper:
when you just want to
merely take advantage
you don't really give a damn
if they sicken or die
you don't care
you don't care what happens
but if you'd learn to love
you would care.
You make me think of rape.
What?
Yes, I said that.

— from *Dial Designates* The Seventies

Short Life

On parts of Leavenworth Street
solid black sidewalks
people with no place to go
are glad to be out and their
happiness thrusts through their skulls
in greetings, in speeches.

There are couples in the Tenderloin
Oh yes there are couples
moving fast with a springy step
wearing clever clothing
savoring every breath
savoring every breath of a short life.

Sixth Street

Locks are laughs to the riffs and raffs
For they have passkeys assorted.
Raff stole my gown and went downtown
How silly they consorted.
Meow, meow is what they're now
Aiming at my window.
Oh if I should ever meet one
Won't I be the sweet one.
Oh where did the funny din go?
I'd laugh and clap and whistle back
If these toughs crack no more than lingo.

Snowwoman

In front of our building
in an alcove like a large fireplace
she spends the night sitting
on a royal blue plastic milk crate
swathing herself in plastic jackets
canvas cloths and wool
sometimes in the morning
sitting there like a doll
with her face covered
no one brings her food and drink
people waiting for the bus ignore her
threesomes of people talk in the cold
ignoring her territory
as if she were no one
or merely a snowwoman
in a snow and ice landscape

Taylor Street

There's little here for my delight
unless the wet footprints of the rain
where a breeze lifts from gritty pavement
smelling of sand and stones delights me
somewhat. And I am free as air is breathed,
American, ready to kiss or kill
or arbitrate on behalf of peace.
And that is my walk down Taylor Street.
And that is my wish down Taylor Street.
And that is my will down Taylor Street.
And that is my way down Taylor Street.
And that is my whip down Taylor Street.

C i t y

Rows upon rows of buildings ascend the street
housewives and grandmas scurry by
with baskets of meats
with shameful self-propulsion
people go by in cars
the earth is covered with concrete
the earth is imprisoned in tars
here and there a tree or shrub, but
we are ripe for wars!
>   The folks go down to the Metro
>   wrinkled with petty fears
>   not one of them is worth the sweat
>   that bothered engineers.
The earth is full of tubing
of water and sewage and wires
the Metro races underneath
carrying fools and liars!
>   Mama sleeps in a doorway
>   but her bedroll stays unrolled
>   Bart sleeps in a parking lot
>   with cardboard to keep out cold
Cecil prepares a sermon
that includes the winos and nuts
>   these beg from me my penny
>   but I pass — glad that St Anthony
>   feeds guts of nuts, winos and sluts
>   let them hunt down cigarette butts.
No one is very good looking
dwarfed men and bawdy hags
file tiredly down the downtown streets
in our polyester rags (include me)
>   Today not one rich satyr
>   The meat rack boys just loiter.
>   Where are the bankers and earls?
>   Where are the pretty girls?

Close to Home

The fashion floor at Macy's smelling of moth wings
pressed, white, dried and the essential butterfly
probing antennae mislead to the flowers of dresses
blooming, the great streaked artist's shout
imprisoned on dresses — silent carpet, mute shoes

Seventh Street, I walk down it at 5:45AM
to see the sunrise magnificent polluted with
smokestacks, clouds like paste dirty orange and white
the industrial calls attention to itself like a horn.

Downtown Strolls

I like to hear the cars go by
fixed with a bass stereo
I stare about elaborately curious
of the sound and find it oh
in the low slung car. There are
men inside celebrating
high on the low sounds
expressing a unique element
achieved by electronics.
Conqueror sounds! you set such goals
of sensual happiness
for my downtown strolls.

A Young Black Girl at the BART Station

That old woman sitting on the concrete block
Her hair white and gray, her clothes nice
If I sit behind her on my back and
Raise my fine dark legs with the running shoes
I can kick her. I do it. Kick, kick, kick.
She won't do anything, she can't do anything.
Oh her train is here, and when she left
She called me nigger under her breath.

Asian Girl at the Bus Stop

That fat man likes me. Rolls of fat
On his neck above the collar. Bald head
Gray tailored trousers, navy blue blazer —
I think he likes me, following and talking.
I'll marry him. Then I'll be a citizen;
I'll bring him cigars, I'll cook him
Roast beef with the fat, lamb with lamb fat,
Potatoes with cheese, desserts
With whipped cream every day,
Booze. While I eat rice and noodles
He will have heart attack.
I will have his house, all his possessions,
Properties. I know my way is slow,
But he will love me, too.

James Chin

James Chin delights me
here is where he's been
to Sacramento and New York
to see our Lady Liberty
presented to the world.
James has a marvelous snoot
an aristocratic nose
someone in his ancestry
must have gone to Rome.
James used all his SSI check
to regale Lady Liberty,
that's patriotic
and kind of cute.
Somewhat an artist and a psychic
he attaches like a sidekick.
I'd love to see again
his merry eyes, angular build
and hear from him how he
spent his youth in Mainland China.
James phoned me up saying
"Hello. I want to take
your panties down."
He sure spoke frankly,
but I hung up the phone.
He appeared much later
with a new stocky physique,
a changed appearance.
This time he hoped for
lots of money. I don't
miss him anymore. except . . .

San Francisco Zoo's Malay Bear

With orange moons under his chin
This guy's decked out for a scene
Better than this. The Philippine bear
Pivots his head from one shoulder to
The other like a Balinese. His Pooh Legs
Stretched out, he sits serenely on
His rump, exposing his Neat Penis.
He's got all day to look at the likes
Of us. He tilts his chin with a
Blacklipped tightlipped philosophical
Smile . . . He's got all day . . . . . and
We "flip" out . . . staring into each other's eyes.

Peaches

A dollar thirty nine is almost an entire
Skid Row meal still there they are
small regular good in cellophane
Dried Peaches from San Rafael
a dollar thirty nine
they suit me well.

Two oh two is what they cost along with
Knudsens bottled juice, two oh two well spent.
I don't know when I have felt so good as when
drinking this clean juice and eating
These Dried Peaches

The Derelict of the Walk

Foot traffic coming the other way
Straight as an arrow, going somewhere
Except the derelict, traveling at angles
From side to side, weaving, faltering.
He is mine. A human being, a human being
All mine. I want to stop him and give him
A hug. I'll kiss him. I didn't. What
Would have happened if I hugged
And kissed the derelict of the walk?
My human being. I am hungry for one.

Star Children

"I got to go to church
not the Thieves Church but — "
"Where is the Thieves Church?"
"Oh it's up there that way"
"I went to church yesterday,
I went to St. Pat's,
now they have confession in
three Filipino dialects — "
"Who is their Father?"
"I don't know.
I only been there once."
"My pastor is Father O'Donnell
at Guadalupe Church.
Guadalupe is our Patroness.
That's the first time the Virgin
appeared in the Americas —
in Mexico City."

"Oh, was she a Virgo?"

A real conversation at 7th Street, 1978

St. Anthony's

Down, Hitler Heart
Do not anticepticize this scene
with your purifying schema
Let them live
If you're a giver, give
> *Let the misfits proclaim*
> *the glory of God*
> *All over the earth*
> *Let the crippled and insane*
> *show you what God can do*
> *and What You Almost Became*
These folks in line
could be like you,
Without food and fashion
what good would you do?
> Let us therefore see them
> Let all know them
> Let us see you

Hairless

This is being done fast.
It's over between us except for my response
This wounded bird still flaps its wings
This paralyzed foot attempts to walk.
He demands I bow out gracefully
but I whimper to him. Inside
I imagine a sharp glass tear
from some imagined chandelier. I crack.
All he says is that I should be nice about it.

I started this: I left him dry
I took our children, the apples of my eye
I left a note. He did not know of this moving day
or that I had another man that day until I told him
and we laughed. I only needed to do that to know I
preferred you, I said. But he would not join us.

Perfidia, perfidio, we had been married in Mexico
because my first marriage was still binding in the
states.
Prior to the pain and rejection
I shaved my head. Tired of my straight bleached
blond hair.
My scalp of short prickles I covered with a cap.
It must be remembered that he was calculating
the worth of a woman bald, compared to
his black handsome head. "Women like me,
think me good," he said.

In 1959, no females were in fashion without hair.
Punk women nearly unknown, only in Africa
or later, Star Trek, womens shaved heads revealed.

Tottering

We're already dead at 50
but allowed to keep feeding our corpses
have heart's desires,
work at a typewriter.
Look down the parabola
of the past; isn't it
all there, beginning, end
mistake rectification
stumble success? Offspring?
Then live knowing you've died
mourn yourself, make music
of tragedy and longing,
longing for life.
Boo! I know that's you
with your wormy blood

The Daydream

For Dean Lipton, 1919 - 1992

A pigeon swims on the warm brick
its legs curled under.
Wondering if it is hurt I
wonder at my tenderness!

Would I be tender if a hungry mist
dissolved these many people here
the sun   evaporate them and
an upward wind swirl them away?

No, but I'd want one left, one for love
and friendship. And knowledge. Who? Who?

Dean Lipton waiting in a little brown
doorway
of a little brown house!

*Dean: A newspaper man and novelist and president
of the San Francisco Writers Workshop for thirty years.*

Going Against the Light

We were going against the light
through snow etched deeply by muddy
footprints other than ours. The sky
was broken up minutely as if
containing curling flesh in hundreds of
separations illuminated by red and redgold
borders. It was the day we began
at sunset to own the turf together
to commit our lives to this sorry
friendship — clouds of flesh weeping
blood — and see sideways how frail
the person we were committing with
we two abandoned and hopeless
but after Im Gegegenlicht — "Going Against
the Light" — how sunny the electric light
for dinner and bed, how dear our youthful
resources being counted like sunlight
into our pretend cans of film.

Surreal for Jack Micheline

Jack: 1928 - 1998

You counseled the young
with your wings of almond
your feet were flagships
for others to follow.
> You uplifted the prairie dog
> to a new status
> you uplifted the prairie

You smelled truth
with your nose of turquoise
melodies ran off your behind
and down your legs of diamond

Real for Jack

You read aloud for the
rapture of men and women
you knew the arts, you were a painter
people came to your readings
You took noodles and ketchup
and made a rare spaghetti

About Jack

As a kid he had had his own
book that he wrote
placed with the other books
in the public library of his city
When he grew up he had heavy hair on his head
and an overcoat like worn by Mafiosi
seen in one of his rare photographs.
He went to Spain on an inheritance from a relative.
He lost his wife to the mayor of the town.
As a young man he wrote a novel *In the Bronx*
and had it printed in Holland.

Micheline Lovers

The young chicks of poetry
peppered the gathering at Jack's memorial
in their black leotards
Jack's voice resounding on tape
Jack Micheline of Rumania and New York
died in California, his father's state
I am filled with thoughts of his worth
like a hallelujah. I envy those who mourn.

My Father Killed Outdoors in the Morning

This death seems like some awful thing
That was always true. Gross violence directed
Unkindly at you   A petty hope for a Twenty
Dollar Bill or two   The theft of keys so that
They could do what you usually do — drive
Your car.   Oh it seems to have happened
Before our time began   Man being chased
By the Satanic man   And if my grief were
Born a million years ago   How much further
Does it have to go   My mother's tears are
Timely, and yet they flow   As if they were
Turned on long ago   I cannot remember when
I did not know   murder and loss   the Battlefield
Lively once   I remember   now barren
And the Soldier gone; this is in Time   the children's
Anger turning to caring for one another.

July 1982

In Memoriam

I weep for all black women who died young
because this society was too demanding of them
who were correct, ambitious and in pursuit
of ideals manifest, of the highest norms
and white ones, I do not know their names
Karen Carpenter on her drums, died young

I weep blood for Glenda who was kind
smiling and with her own particular grace
calm, aware and quick to comfort; yesterday
she heard me on the phone seeking clinics
for my friend, and smiling delivered to me
Gene Coleman's big directory regarding help
for persons suffering substance abuse.
I planned to thank her just last night
Today she bled to death after a hysterectomy.
I want to point out that she was black,
a responsible person who died young!

Act of Dying

So all the power in a voice across the room
And image, seeming fixed as the world
Is cancelled, local now, by the act of dying.
Then we are our small selves, our power drawn back
Into us, part of the destruction. For the living,
Sorrow. A pause. Again sorrow and pauses
Throughout the day of mourning our loss.

Tenderness

I will think of Sharon — I have willed it
When I see flowers, fruits or snow
And if I ever see waterlilies
Crowding against a shore
Or spread like stepping stones
Across a pond, and hear
The tiny hums of small insects
In their windblown life
Or see a painting of these things
I will to think of her
Who left us moved
To dark uncomfortable passions
At her death in 1997
And against our collective will is gone forever.

James Coburn

Eyes protected
Mouth protected
By his flesh of spice
And his spicy breath

To a Woman

your smiles
when you have something
good to say, are loveliness
warm as the coffee freckles
I shun you for your bad temper
and refusal to acknowledge
The Other or let them speak

Grandma In The Giftwrap Line

"There shouldn't be a store like this
rolls of paper, wood and oil wasted
yet I come here, I buy here.

"Kiss of death for wood and oil
paper rolls and printed bags
yet I come here, I buy here.

"Toys, Toys. Proliferating toys.
Too many toys and too many shoppers.
Why all this to simply let them know
we love them? A toy a year. A toy
a week. Each day. Waste, worthless.
Yet here I am. I come and buy here."

Reno

it's humorous to see
money in buckets all the
trips going off, noise
and a winner with his
rainbow and pots. he's
nonchalant, and going to
play back all he's got.
all year we reckon money
for real. we come here
to play with it regardless
of

The Kiss

spare, sparrow, spare!
spare, sparrow, spare!
around his mouth is
sparrow hair, spined
to prick aside my lip
like a match strikes.
a chin I imagined
will shove my jawbone
into the future where he is.
he is all future
because he is an artist.
all this was wove
torn out and begun again
because I beheld him
like a bird's nip incising
and feathers brushing
at the same time all words
exacted some smiles

Rain

looks like a
muddy footprint or
a bad photograph out there.
The fountain shoots gray water.
spreads puddles of milk.
Milk-black cars trundle or
are parked. The trees are brackish in the air
the very mud green
color of despair.
>   But lights within the building
>   are fair, each room a universe
>   with suns: or candled lair
>   city workforce is working there.

The Typewriter

Joking at the counter with a joke
like a fanny-pat
the pencilled planner pursues a problem. The folk
dance is soon over, the paragraph unfat.
The right word is spoken.
Julia speaks it.
Now my rhythm is unbroken
and the little pieces fit.
She says, One rolls up each line
to a fit so fine
it looks technical
produced by the mind's telling.
Then she says, Watch your spelling.
You'll never be able to make a correction.
We tried twice, and had a lovely chart.

The White Serpent

Do you have a cigarette miss? God bless you.
I need a light. She walked away, she's by a bole
of a tree, trying to light hers out of the wind,
now stepping into a doorway, and in that 90 degree
angle she's beat the wind. I'll wait for somebody
with matches. I was thinking about the white
serpent when I saw Lady fishing one smoke
out of her thick glossy pack, and then I wanted
to taste the serpent more than I'd want a quarter
more than the Lady's dollars. Feels good
to get something from her freely.

Serpent spits mind poison, makes you
bend over and pick it up when it's been trailed
on the street or a long butt my tongue and
palate love the dizzy warmth the sucked breaths
feels better than food the white serpent
is a sweet sleep I don't want to eat

Can I see your lighter Bro?
Crawling away in search of a light
holding the sun cigarette new chalky up
now in shadow now in sunlight
the white serpent needle bright

The Third Baptist Church

Dear Lord Thy
Sunday Geese, Thy Virgins
Wearing Floppy Hats or Turbans
Of Wrapped White Net, Of Satin
In Satinedged Coats. Dear God, Cotton
Would Suit Me but Wool Net and Satin
And not a One of Cotton here this Morning.
Dear Jesus I want one too
A White Hat and White Coat to Greet You.

The Scalding

old tragic waking
in white plastic clothesline
self-choking at neck
I don't want to go out door
did I fail to breathe?
      stone limbs entangled
      representing my sins
      desperation. such despair
      to see people, any people.
      is blood sugar low?
disentangling limbs
life surges once more
sin consciousness gone
      walking across room
      happiness courses through
      I rejoice a little.
the day brings pie
and earrings at Macy's
because I thought she left
I cleaned it up slowly
      discount cigarettes
      Rosemary whom I abandon
      our coffee burned my hands
      after a siege of Parkinsons.
I went to the little store
lemonade.   a can of lemonade.
but need to eat now.
she does not know of the scalding
I have not told her or pursued her
      bought smoked clams for hunger
      sorry to lose Rosemary
      her visit intrusive at lunchtime.
      hot coffee on red hands
      perhaps she'll visit again?

The Siskiyous

The Siskiyous are sisterly
and very near my history
of Christmasy treeeys dense
as panther fur — I won't go further
I'll look for her here (Dunsmuir)

The Dewdrop and the Petal

The drop of dew
has a hundred eyes
and little cellular
interstices that reflect
like spit
more beautiful than me
or my spit
and the petal
is softer than
silk blend clothes!

Palm Prints

plump palm prints of sunlight
pigeons are trailing louis the XIV gowns
a pinch of cornbread, a pinch of popcorn
among the recycled waste on the grounds.

the sun's palms grasp the city, the tremulous weather
pushes to be invited in. people in painful appraisal
or practical praise or pouring assent, the streets
the plazas — pleasing even in pain.

Winter Freeze

The trees on McAllister Street
Were bare but poles have sprung out
And bear signs in cold air.
Further down the street toward Downtown
Five new trees, named Bottlebrush.
One has a red brush with small yellow stars.
This brush would clean a babyfood jar.
The trees speak of their feminine fancy leaves
As we breathe them in. Hush
Their nodding branch ends and glorious
gray-green catwillow-soft leaves.

At the Presidio of San Francisco, Little Poem

In a dell of redwood trees
the floor like a woven
feather bed
the young trees scarred
by fire

Arboretum

Blase of nature's charms
I enjoy the wind
cooling my arms.

Further into the Arboretum
Father Nature —I feel I meet him.
Leaves and buds of precious make
enchant with art.

Burdens of anger and money
lifted from people
who fit shrinking into the wind's
sharp prankster pull.

Two New England Memories

1.

Once I knew an Atlantic that fell like
Green glass, a long mesa — table — with
An immaculate frill, and the glass
Gathered, and did not shatter
But was blown to a rim.
Outside Manchester I saw the water
Sleeping like a poodle — curly
Indents on the water's surface —
where children walked among
The dry and fishy dishes that were
Shells

2.

When I first saw Greater Boston
There was sunlight on dusty leaves
In a cradle of trees in the delicate
Strain of morning. There was a
Heralding in a sign from a single
Sunbeam. I thought I had come upon love.

17 Mile Drive

The land forms lips
at ocean's edge
Lips are drinking
drinking and losing
        Houses near the sea
        are small and snug
        kissing the ground

Listen by the bus
to the Great Mother the sea
to Grandmother the land
        The land accepts the
        kisses of the sea

Dalmatian hills of
cream sand
doused with charcoal-
colored foliage
and red ice plants
        Next to them the black soil
        flat as a table, accepting
        seeds   (None would call
        ice plants weeds.)

The Hollow

A gray bridge made of planks
inches close to water
water in an oval, only a
few leaves float. February
with brown leaves. only one bright
one floating yellow and green.
      Skater bugs dapple water quickly
      hesitate, then change pattern
      skating on surface only.
The Green Leaf is so big
shaped like a canoe,
I think it's my poems
floating alone on water
ugly size and overripe fruit
inedible banana.
      Partially submerged it is not moving
      at one time it moved because
      it should have been under a tree
      and is not. A Leaf that is my poems
      dominating the brown pond.

Three Theaters

in four directions from Hyde and McAllister
white backdrops   two blocks down buildings
are brown.

across the street from white water-
multishooting fountains, wet brick
the toasted building toasted to char
the dirty yellow buildings scoured
with paint

up Leavenworth and beyond the bank
on Jones utility blanket browns
wrapping people in doorways or
on the street

neighbor commits to color of neighbor

star center a white with a wash of
gold, blue, and gray and gray green
for law, business and granting of
life   marriage

everywhere people endeavor   to travel
to carry their frail merchandise
        of cut down necessity . . .
        to Street Harbor

My Mother Called Last Night

My mother called last night. My father was with her.
The following may be a delusion. My parents are
dead. The room was full of smoke.

I was in bed. I heard and saw a commotion in the air.
Then I saw the faint silver outlines of my father sitting
on the portopotty and my mother straddling his lap.
She was facing him. I could barely see them. I more
felt them than saw them.

"Jan," my mother implored. "You've got to help us.
We have no bodies. Help us to get bodies." I had no
idea how to help spirits of the dead get bodies. I felt a
familiar incompetence and sadness. I was failing
them again. I turned my face to the wall. The out-
lines of the spirits of the dead seem to leave by the
window. I turned my face to the wall again, to the
wall's nothingness that could shield my eyes from this
visit of the dead. I miss my parents, but I want them
to stay in their graves.

The Car

They ride around
and cover ground
they spring full fledged at dawn
predictable as a reflex.
They do not cease at noon.
After sunset they're still riding
at least until eleven
the next day —
they ride around again.

The earth give up her metals
the ground give up his sauce
so they can ride around and round
and be the boss of us.

Lovers

When I had lovers before him
we wore social clothes
I loved with who I was
revealed on exams, apps
for work, birth certificate
pants and bra that fit
       But now I love one in a new
       essential and breathtaking way
       Right to the Quick of my Bones
       as animals we are one

       He is ever a mystery to me
       His strange projections the tree
       wearing hair laid flat like a
       mushroom   The burning
       of his life-exposed body
       and the cinders falling
       The bushes of air by my bedside
       His body crawling   He's always moving
       just a step away, hardly within
       a hand's grasp   I lose him and feel him
       again turning and I see his face
muzzled and smiling. He looks at me
and then Mendelssohn smiles
who knew he wrote the SOMERNACHTSMUSIK
Wedding March for someone

Grasslands from a Car

the golden hills roll patiently like beasts
backside to our face now the perky cones
of hilltops   California trees show us
which way the wind has blown   trees
scatter like broccoli in a yellow salad
or march across ridges, bent halfway
at the hiway's edge trees bushing into
the tar.

the car is a geo metro, individual smooth
dynamo   cars line up as dominoes,
go right or left at the intersection
shadows on the road illusory mirrors
reflecting the cars' bottoms or look
like oil spilt

grasslands ending at Yuba City, now there's
corn, tomatoes and peach trees which
extend up their hands covered with hair into the air
grass colored grass wheat colored grass
northeast middle California seen from the geo
my sister driving

The Cider Vat

the apple bough fell in the
        cider vat
the worm didn't see, just
        the parrot
apples, pressed, dyeing orange
acid leaves impart a taste
skimmed off. neighbor told.
he and i sipped thru straws
the green taste of naughty
        leaves that
teach that changes have a
        cause.

Janice King grew up in Oakland, California. In the 50s she was married to George Starbuck and had three children, two of whom live and work in the Bay Area. The third one lives and works in New York City as a commercial writer. She worked for many years at the San Francisco Department of City Planning as a secretary. She has now retired into the loneliness and liberty of the life of writing. Her first book of poems *Burdens of Bliss* was published by Freedom Voices in 1993. She is currently the editor of Autobiography magazine.